THE CHINESE INVENT Gunpowder

John Murphy

CRAZY COOL CHINA

ROSEN PUBLISHING
NEW YORK

SinolinguA
华语教学出版社
BEIJING

Jointly published in 2021 by Sinolingua Co., Ltd., Beijing, China, and
The Rosen Publishing Group, Inc., New York, New York, United States.

First Edition

Editor: John Kemmerer
Cover Designer: Haley Harasymiw
Interior Layout: Rachel Rising

Photo credits: Cover Dana.S/Shutterstock.com; cover, pp. 1, 3–48 (background) Sylfida/Shutterstock .com; cover, p. 1 CkyBe/Shutterstock.com; pp. 4, 8, 12, 16, 20, 24, 28, 32, 34, 38, 40, 42 xpixel/Shutterstock.com; p. 5 David Tadevosian/Shutterstock.com; p. 6 Tanachot Srijam/Shutterstock .com; p. 9 ChWeiss/Shutterstock.com; p. 10 videophoto/E+/Getty Images; p. 11 Chinese woodcut, Famous medical figures, Portrait of Ge Hong/Wellcome Collection/Attribution 4.0 International (CC BY 4.0); p. 13 Florilegius/Alamy Stock Photo; pp. 14, 18 Album/Alamy Stock Photo; pp. 17, 26 CPA Media Pte Ltd/Alamy Stock Photo; p. 21 Wikimedia Commons/File: てつはう(震天雷) .jpg/CC BY-SA 3.0; p. 22 The Picture Art Collection/Alamy Stock Photo; p. 25 ullstein bild Dtl./Getty Images; p. 29 Photo Josse/Leemage/Corbis Historical/Getty Images; p. 30 Heritage Images/Hulton Archive/Getty Images; p. 33 Blaine Harrington III/Alamy Stock Photo; p. 35 Roger Bacon, Stipple engraving/Wellcome Collection/ Attribution 4.0 International (CC BY 4.0); p. 36 Bridgeman Images; p. 39 powerofforever/DigitalVision Vectors/Getty Images; p. 41 © North Wind Picture Archives; p. 43 Feng Li/Getty Images.

Cataloging-in-Publication Data
Names: Murphy, John.
Title: The Chinese invent the gunpowder / John Murphy
Description: New York : Rosen Publishing, 2022. | Series: Crazy cool China | Includes glossary and index.
Identifiers: ISBN 9781499469189 (pbk.) | ISBN 9781499469196 (library bound) | ISBN 9781499469202 (ebook)
Subjects: LCSH: Technology–China–History–Juvenile literature. | Gunpowder–History–Juvenile literature. | Inventions–China–History–Juvenile literature.
Classification: LCC T27.C5 M8772022 | DDC 609.31–dc23

Manufactured in the United States of America

CPSIA Compliance Information: Batch #BSRYA22. For further information contact Rosen Publishing, New York, New York, at 1-800-237-9932.

Contents

Gunpowder:

One of the "Four Great Inventions" of China

Gunpowder was invented by the Chinese in the second century CE. It was the first explosive ever to be developed, and its invention forever changed the way wars were fought. So important was this **innovation** to world history and the rise and fall of nations that it is referred to as one of "the Four Great Inventions" of China.

Gunpowder and the military technology it made possible remained within China for several centuries. It began to spread into the rest of Asia, the Middle East, and Europe through both Silk Road trade and Mongol invasions. Inventors in these regions were soon developing ever-larger and more powerful weapons. Defenses against these weapons also improved. Muskets and thicker-walled fortresses that could withstand the blows of large and heavy cannonballs are just two of the innovations driven by gunpowder.

Yet the development of gunpowder as an explosive substance was accidental. The Chinese inventors who discovered its explosive potential were instead hoping to perfect a **formula** for an **elixir**, or potion, that would provide eternal life to whoever took the medicine. Combining sulfur and the mineral saltpeter to make their potion, they quickly realized that the results were highly **flammable**. If the amount of saltpeter in the mixture was increased, the substance could become not just flammable but explosive, too.

Once the **incendiary** properties of this powder were discovered, the Chinese developed many weapons that would begin to revolutionize warfare, including fire arrows, fire lances, bombs and gun shell explosives, and early guns and cannons.

This form of gunpowder is used in military and hunting rifles.

Fireworks were created by the Chinese over a thousand years ago but continue to dazzle and delight us today.

The first firecrackers were probably pieces of bamboo that were heated by fire. The heat caused air pockets in the bamboo to burst, creating a loud crack. Later, hollow bamboo tubes were stuffed with gunpowder and lit on fire. Eventually, bamboo was replaced with tubes made of red paper. Red is considered a lucky color. Even today, the red paper that remains after the firecracker explosion is saved for a few days to preserve the good luck.

Yet inventors the world over also found peaceful and productive uses for the explosive potential of gunpowder. **Civil engineering** benefited greatly from gunpowder's blasting ability, and projects became much more **ambitious**, ushering in the modern industrialized era. For example, canal building, mining, and railroad construction would initially have been impossible without the use of gunpowder. And, even though other explosive devices and powders are used for blasting now, gunpowder continues to be used today, especially in power tools. And what would any public celebration be without those booming, colorful gunpowder explosions that were also invented by the Chinese—fireworks!

An Accidental Invention

The white crystallized mineral that would form the major component of gunpowder is potassium nitrate, also known as saltpeter. The Chinese had been familiar with saltpeter since the middle of the first century CE, and it soon began to be produced in the provinces of Sichuan, Shanxi, and Shandong.

One ninth-century formula for gunpowder was provided in a Taoist text and accompanied by a vivid example of just how flammable this "medicinal" powder could be: "Some have heated together sulfur, realgar [arsenic disulfide], and saltpeter with honey; smoke and flames result, so that their hands and faces have been burnt, and even the whole house where they were working burned down."

Alchemists in China took a particular interest in the mineral. Alchemy combined **natural philosophy** with early semi-scientific experiments. Alchemists were like early chemists, who sought to create medicines and substances that could achieve both spiritual and physical transformations. For example, alchemists often attempted to turn base metals, like lead, into precious metals, like gold. They also sought to create medicines that could cure all diseases. The Chinese alchemists were using saltpeter, in combination with sulfur, to create different medicines. What they most hoped to create was a potion that would give eternal life to whoever ingested it. They soon discovered that when sulfur and saltpeter were combined, the results could be very flammable. And, when the amount of saltpeter was increased to half or more of the total mixture, they could be downright explosive.

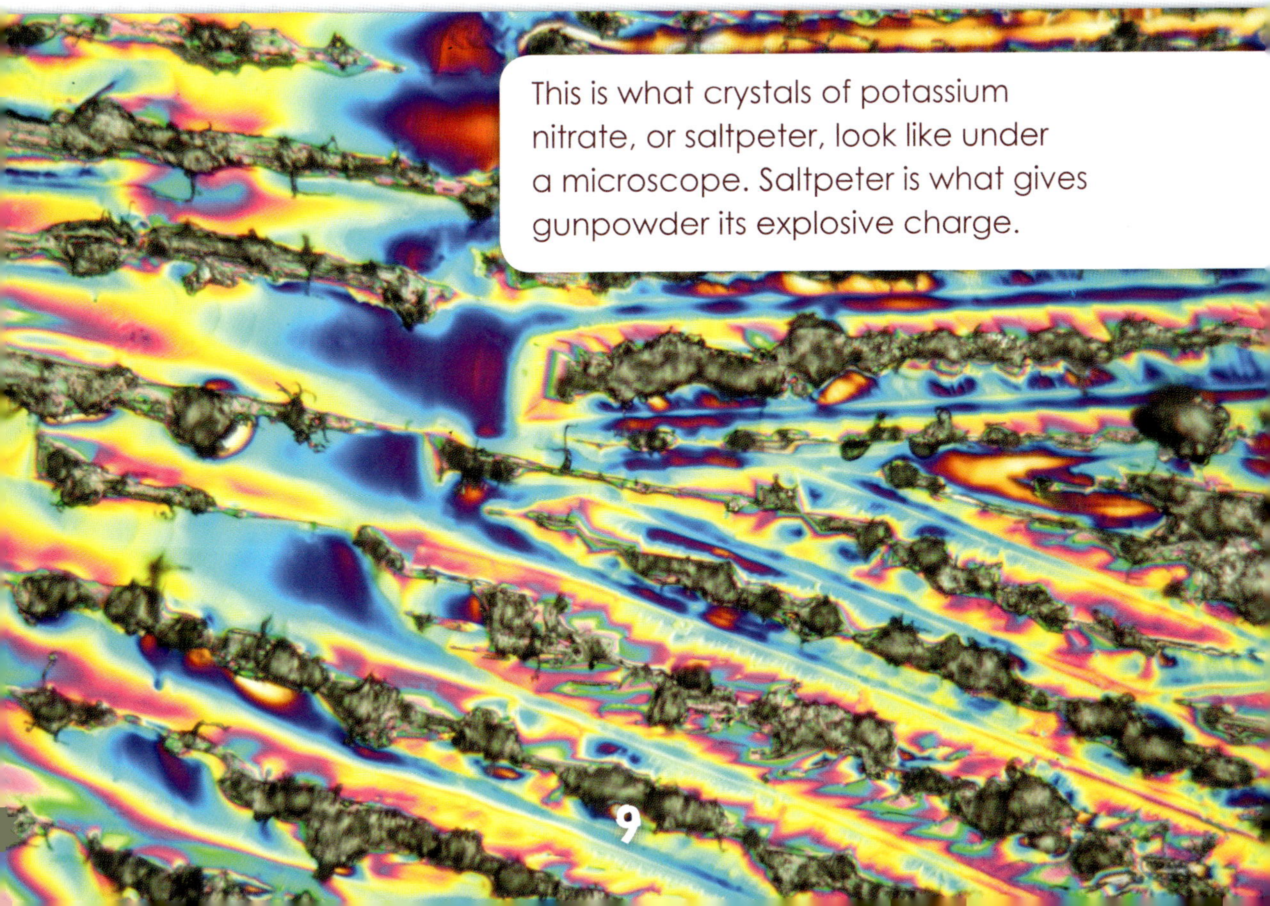

This is what crystals of potassium nitrate, or saltpeter, look like under a microscope. Saltpeter is what gives gunpowder its explosive charge.

Chinese alchemists discovered liquid mercury, or quicksilver, while trying to turn base metals into gold.

The mineral cinnabar was often used in the alchemists' experiments, partly because of its color. Its red tint evoked the sun, royalty, fire, and energy. When cinnabar was roasted, it would liquefy and form a kind of silver known as quicksilver, or mercury.

The earliest reference to a substance that might have been gunpowder was provided in 142 CE by an alchemist named Wei Boyang. He described a combination of three powders that "fly and dance" violently. At the beginning of the fourth century, a Taoist philosopher named Ge Hong listed the ingredients for an explosive powder he had been experimenting with: saltpeter, charcoal, and pine resin.

The philosopher Ge Hong listed the ingredients for gunpowder in the fourth century CE.

Finally, in 808 CE, the first precise formula for what can be considered an early non-explosive form of gunpowder was recorded by a Taoist priest: six parts sulfur to six parts saltpeter to one part birthwort herb. Gunpowder had officially been invented!

Weaponizing "Fire Medicine"

The Chinese word for what would become gunpowder is *huoyao*, or "fire medicine." Though first developed for medicinal purposes, the extreme flammability of the powder soon made others imagine alternative military uses for it.

The eleventh-century-CE Chinese military encyclopedia titled *Wujing Zongyao* (in English, *Collection of the Most Important Military Techniques*) describes how to construct and use a fire arrow: "Behind the arrowhead, wrap up some gunpowder with two or three layers of soft paper, and bind it to the arrow shaft in a lump shaped like a pomegranate. Cover it with a piece of hemp cloth, tightly tied and sealed fast with molten pine resin. Light the fuse, and then shoot it off from a bow."

The first mention of a military use for non-explosive gunpowder seems to be in 904 CE, when the eastern Chinese kingdom of Southern Wu was attacking the city of Nanchang. An officer named Zheng Fan ordered his troops to let loose "flying fire" on one of the city's gates. Once the gate was burning, the troops jumped over the flames, rushed through the breach, and captured the city. Zheng Fan was badly burned during the action but survived and was rewarded with a promotion for his bravery.

Among the ancient Chinese weapons shown here are a fire starter engine (#14) and an explosive gunpowder wagon (#16).

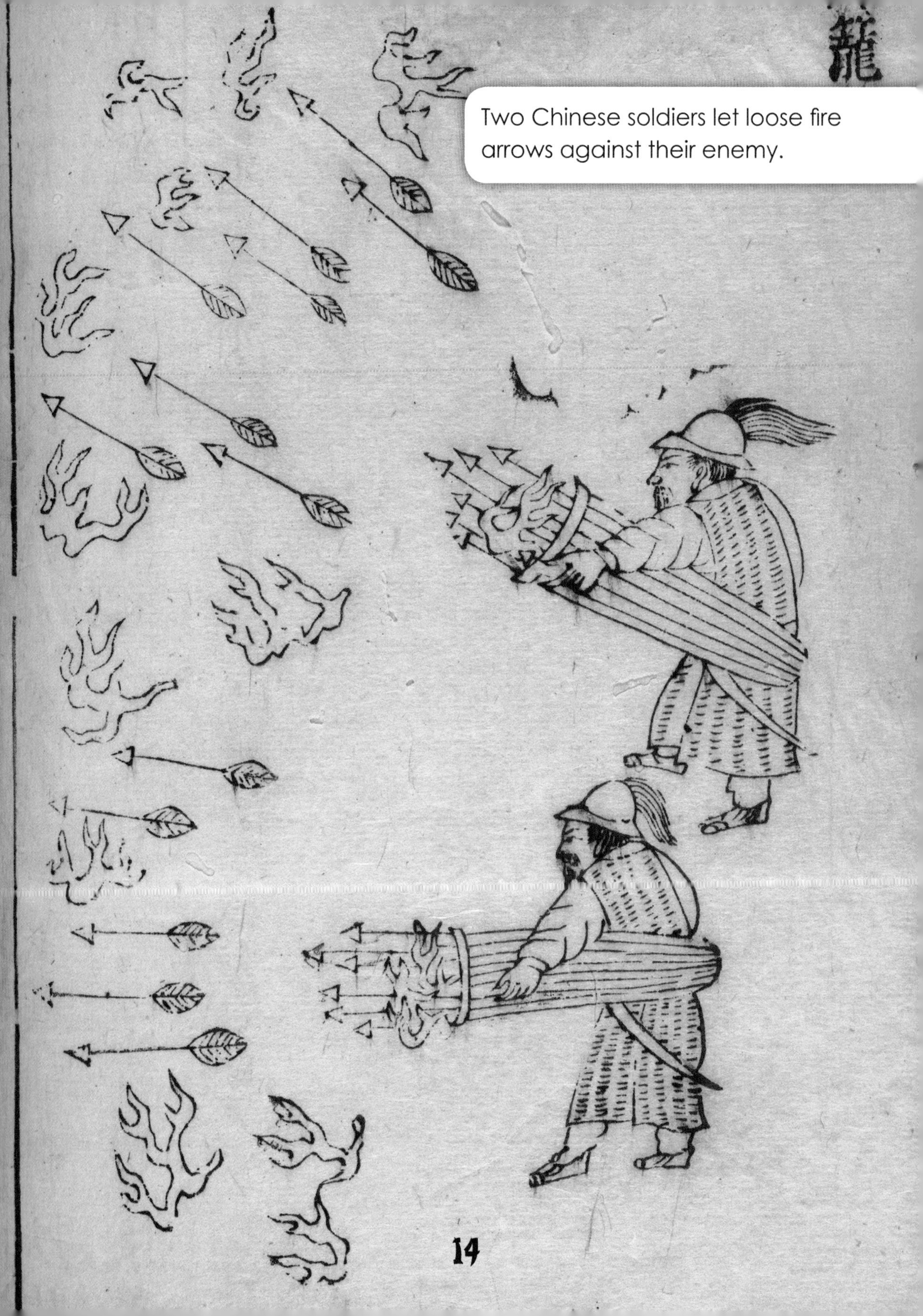

Two Chinese soldiers let loose fire arrows against their enemy.

Later in the tenth century, fire arrows began to be fired from gunpowder tubes rather than from bows. In effect, fire arrows were now rocket-propelled. This new weapon was shown to the emperor of the Song Dynasty in 970. Five years later, a special unit of the Song army, trained in the use of fire arrows, used the gunpowder-propelled fire arrows to destroy the fleet of the enemy empire to the south, the Southern Tang.

The story of this attack does not make it clear exactly what form this "flying fire" took. Many historians believe that what was launched against the city gate were probably "fire arrows." These were arrows that had a bag of gunpowder incendiaries attached to them. They would be fired from a bow or a crossbow. The rush of oxygen that is created when an arrow flies through the air would have intensified the flame produced by the gunpowder, increasing the destruction once it hit its target. The bag or pouch that held the gunpowder supplied additional oxygen to the flames, making them far harder to put out. Also in use at this time were gunpowder pots (a sort of non-explosive fire bomb) that spewed large amounts of fire.

Gunpowder had been weaponized in China, but the weaponry was still incendiary only. Before long, it would also be explosive—and far more deadly.

Explosive Developments

The Song Dynasty took a huge interest in gunpowder technology and encouraged military inventors to create new weapons and share their innovations with the imperial court. When the emperor was shown a weapon that he liked, he ordered that the plans for its making and instructions for its use be made available to all military forces throughout the empire. At the same time, the emperor tried to prevent the technology from spreading to his enemies. His subjects were forbidden from trading sulfur and saltpeter beyond Song borders.

In the eleventh century, the Song court began to recognize the military importance of gunpowder. As a result, in order to stockpile the necessary ingredients and to prevent enemy kingdoms from acquiring gunpowder, the Song court banned much of the trade in saltpeter and sulfur. Alchemists used sulfur in many of their elixirs, and saltpeter was considered a flavor enhancer, like our modern-day table salt. It was especially forbidden to sell these substances to "foreigners"—anyone living beyond the Song territory.

The Song greatly increased the production of gunpowder and fire arrows, creating a huge weapons manufacturing facility in the city of Kaifeng. At about this time, military inventors seem to have taken a great step forward. At some point, someone created a new formula for gunpowder that included more than 50 percent saltpeter. When the amount of saltpeter was increased, the gunpowder went from being merely flammable to highly explosive. There were now a wide variety of gunpowder in use, some probably incendiary and others explosive. They went by the names "blinding powder," "flying powder," "violent powder," "poison powder," "bruising and burning powder," and "smoke-screen powder."

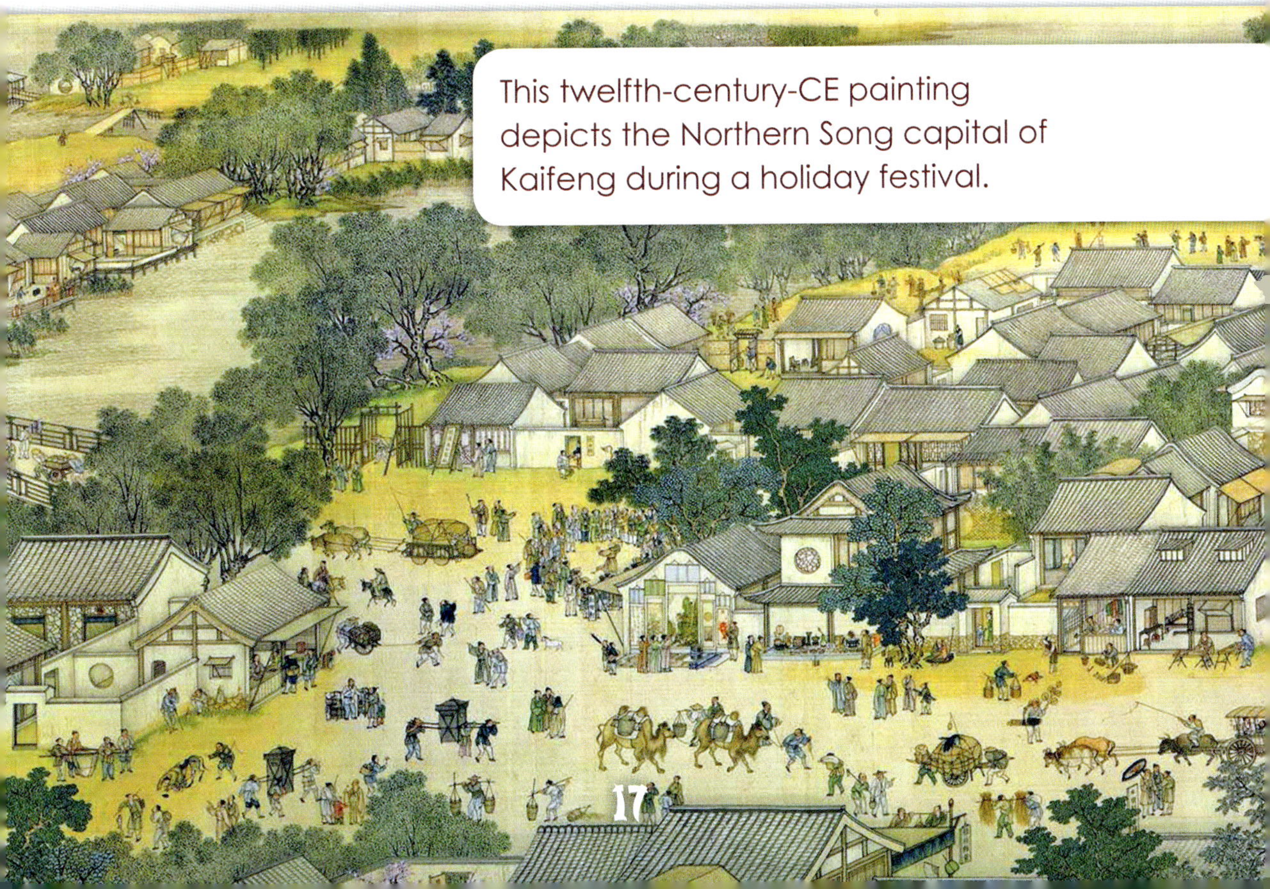

This twelfth-century-CE painting depicts the Northern Song capital of Kaifeng during a holiday festival.

This illustration shows a revolving wheel explosive device that appears to release both fire and projectiles. One is mounted on a horse, and another is fired by a soldier.

A fourteenth-century military manual, the *Huolongjing* (in English, *Fire Dragon Manual*), describes the use of gunpowder in chemical weapons, as well as explosive devices. Added to the usual sulfur, saltpeter, and charcoal were tung oil, urine, ammonia, dung, and scallion juice. These substances would be heated and then spread on broken pieces of porcelain or iron pellets, which would then be packed into an explosive bomb. These chemical bombs were called "divine gunpowder," "poison gunpowder," and "blinding and burning gunpowder."

Wujing Zongyao, an eleventh-century military encyclopedia, lists a number of new weapons, possibly developed for use with the newly explosive gunpowder. It is not clear if all of these weapons were real or just imaginary, but the list includes a "flying incendiary club for subjugating demons," a "caltrop fire ball," a "ten-thousand fire flying sand magic bomb," a "big bees nest," a "burning heaven fierce fire unstoppable bomb," and "fire bricks" that release "flying swallows," "flying rats," "fire birds," and "fire oxen."

Whether these weapons were imaginary or not, incendiary or explosive, history shows that the new saltpeter-rich gunpowder would soon give rise to guns, cannons, and bombs that were all too real.

Fire Lances, Fire Bombs, and Hard Shell Explosives

Early in the twelfth century CE, the Song formed an alliance with the newly established Jin Dynasty of Manchuria in northeast China. The Song and Jin defeated their common enemy, the Liao Dynasty. Soon after, however, they began fighting each other. Gunpowder would play an important role in the Jin-Song Wars.

The Song used rocket-like fire arrows against their former friends. They also used a new and more deadly

During the Jin's siege of Qizhou, the Song army had 3,000 fire bombs, 17,000 fire arrows, and 20,000 "great leather bombs" on hand to defend themselves. At the Jin's siege of Kaifeng in 1126, the Song resisted with "fire bombs [that] fell like rain, and their arrows were so numerous as to be uncountable." There are also references to the Song's use of "molten metal bombs." According to witnesses, anything these bombs came into contact with would disintegrate completely.

weapon—the fire lance. The fire lance is considered one of the earliest examples of a gun. It was a spear that initially had a flamethrower attached to it. Later developments allowed it to fire **projectiles** through a paper or bamboo tube. Fire lances were used to destroy the wooden **siege** engines the Jin were using to attack the walls of De'an during the siege of that city in 1132.

Both the Song and the Jin were also hurling fire bombs at each other. These were incendiary only, and they included lime to create blinding smoke screens. These were used on land and at sea, with the Song navy using them often against Jin ships.

These ceramic bombs belonged to a wrecked ship that was part of the Mongol armada of Kublai Khan. He attempted to conquer Japan in the thirteenth century.

This drawing of Chinese fire ships appears in the eleventh-century military manual called *Wujing Zongyao*. The ships were used as floating incendiaries against enemy navies.

When the Jin were attacking Kaifeng, they were surprised and thrown into confusion and panic by a Song weapon they may not have been prepared for—the "thunderclap bomb." These bombs were made by mixing pieces of broken porcelain with gunpowder. The mixture was packed in a bamboo tube and placed within a round casing. The casing itself was also covered with gunpowder. The thunderclap bomb was said to make Jin troops flee in terror.

It was the Jin, however, who may have increased the explosive and deadly potential of gunpowder. They invented an iron-encased bomb. Because it had an iron coating, the bomb was required to be explosive, not merely incendiary, in order to be effective. It had to detonate and explode, in order to break through the iron casing. Following the explosion, the broken pieces of iron became deadly weapons themselves. This new weapon, first used in the siege of the fortress city of Qizhou, may have helped the Jin turn the tide against the Song. The Song did not have these cast iron bombs, and they were now outgunned. The Song fell to the Jin in 1127 and lost control of the north of China. The Jin had risen to power, thanks in no small part to the explosive force of gunpowder.

The First Firearm

Early fire lances shot flames, but they did not fire projectiles. They were **pyrotechnic** devices whose light, flame, smoke, and noise were used to startle and intimidate the enemy. A bamboo or reusable paper tube would be packed with gunpowder and attached to a spear. A long fuse would be lit and ignite the gunpowder, and the flames would shoot forth toward the spearhead. Eventually, more explosive gunpowder was used, and

The oldest known handgun, or "hand cannon," is the "Xanadu gun," made in 1298. It was found in the ruins of Xanadu, the famed Mongol summer palace. It is just over a foot long (34 cm) and weighs about 13.5 pounds (6 kg). It can be dated so precisely because it has an inscription that includes the era name and date, as well as a serial number and manufacturing information. This suggests that many other guns like it were being made at the same time.

projectiles—like broken pieces of ceramic or iron pellets—were added to the flame-throwing tube or barrel. This new and improved lance was known as a flying fire lance. In general, a flying fire lance could be fired only once, and the projectiles could travel only about 10 feet (3 m).

The first true bullet to be fired from a fire lance was invented around 1259 when a pellet was packed into a bamboo barrel. The wad occluded, or fully blocked, the barrel, so when the gunpowder's explosion pushed it out of the lance, the result was an eruption of great force and noise.

Chinese soldiers launch flying fire lances packed with projectiles against an enemy fortress.

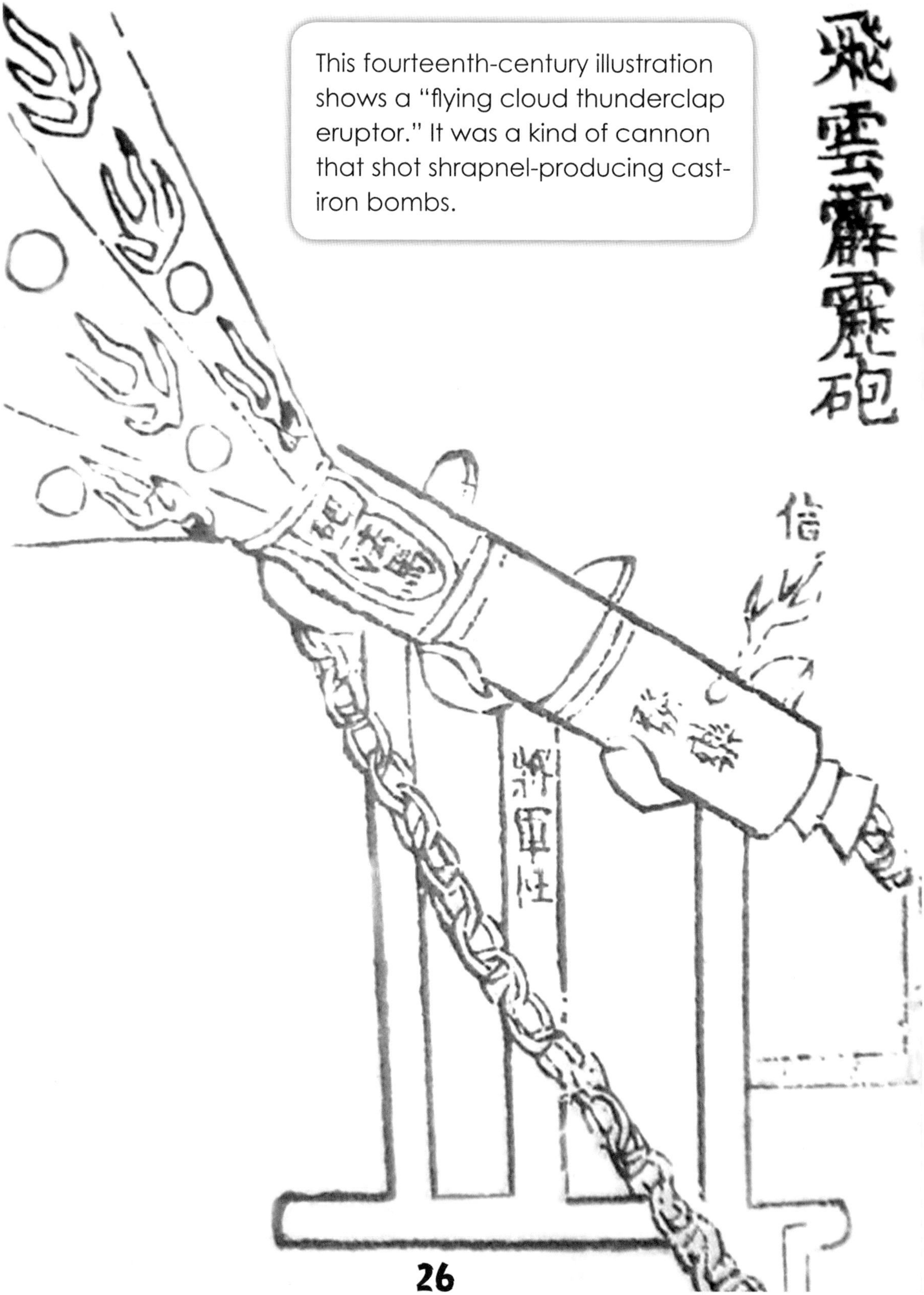

This fourteenth-century illustration shows a "flying cloud thunderclap eruptor." It was a kind of cannon that shot shrapnel-producing cast-iron bombs.

The Wuwei Bronze Cannon is the largest thirteenth-century Chinese gun, or cannon, to be discovered. It weighs 238 pounds (108 kg) and is 3 feet (100 cm) long. When found in Wuwei in northwest China, it still contained a little gunpowder in its barrel, or muzzle. It also contained an iron ball about 3 inches (8 cm) in diameter. The cannon's muzzle, however, could fit a ball as large as almost 5 inches (12 cm) in diameter.

The next great innovation occurred just seventeen years later, when metal barrels were first introduced. Bamboo fire lances could be used only once. They were destroyed by the gunpowder explosion. Large piles of them had to be on hand during battles. And, though the paper barrels—made of seventeen layers of paper—were reusable, metal barrels were far more durable. Once they were adopted, the spear portion of the fire lance was no longer used. The metal-barreled lances began to be called "eruptors." They were used to shoot out broken pieces of porcelain and ceramic shards, metal pellets, sand, and poisonous gas and chemicals.

At this point, what was once the fire lance had become a weapon we would recognize as an early kind of gun, or "hand cannon."

The Mongols and Gunpowder

For hundreds of years, gunpowder and the weapons and military technology it made possible stayed within China. It is not clear exactly how knowledge and use of gunpowder began to spread beyond China. But, beginning in the middle of the thirteenth century, written references to gunpowder began appearing throughout Asia, the Middle East, and Europe. Actual **firearms** did not begin appearing in these places until the fourteenth century.

It is possible that the Mongols used captured Jin weapons or the knowledge and skills of captured Jin weapon-makers in their future fights. When the Mongols turned their attention to the Song Dynasty to the south, it is believed that they brought fire arrows, fire lances, and fire bombs to the fight, including molten metal bombs. The Mongol army also came to include hundreds of thousands of soldiers experienced in the use of gunpowder weaponry.

One theory for how gunpowder and guns began to spread beyond China is that they were carried throughout Eurasia by the Mongol invasions. The Mongols, the founders of the Yuan Dynasty, would have encountered and used gunpowder weapons during their conquests of the Song and Jin in the thirteenth century. During a siege of the Jin capital of Kaifeng, the Mongols met with resistance in the form of fire arrows, flying fire lances, and explosives called "heaven-shaking thunder bombs." These bombs may have been encased in iron, because they are described as producing **shrapnel** that could penetrate armor and kill soldiers and horses standing a great distance from the explosion. Those standing near the explosion were said to turn into ash.

Genghis Khan was the leader of the largest empire in world history. In the thirteenth century, the Mongol Empire stretched from Europe to Japan, and from Siberia to India.

The Mongols battle the Jin in northern China in 1211 CE. This illustration is from a fifteenth-century history of the Mongols.

Both the Song and the Jin made explosive last stands against the Mongols. After the Jin emperor committed suicide in 1234, ending the dynasty, one of his loyal warriors gathered all the metal he could find, even gold and silver, to make metal bombs to use against the Mongols in one last desperate fight. In 1277, some doomed Song warriors built a huge iron suicide bomb that killed them and many of their Mongol enemies.

It is thought that the Mongols used some kind of gunpowder weapons against the Jin, but they were said to be uncharacteristically fearful of the flying fire lance and "heaven-shaking thunder bomb." Seemingly outgunned, the Mongols nevertheless conquered the Jin Dynasty in 1234. They would conquer the Song Dynasty in 1279.

Some accounts of the Mongol invasions of eastern Europe in the first half of the thirteenth century mention the use of bomb-hurling catapults and flamethrowers. Stories and visual depictions of the Mongol invasions of Japan later in the century describe metal-encased shrapnel bombs. So it does seem possible that the Mongol invasions provided at least one pathway for gunpowder and weaponry to begin spreading around the world.

Gunpowder Travels the Silk Road

Another theory for how gunpowder spread outward from China throughout the rest of Asia, the Middle East, and Europe involves the Silk Road. This was a network of trade routes—both land and sea—that wound throughout East Asia, Southeast Asia, South Asia, Persia (Western Asia), East Africa, the Arabian Peninsula, and Southern Europe. It is named for silk, which was its most important trade good, exported from China beginning in the 200s CE during the Han Dynasty.

Religion also journeyed along the Silk Road. Chinese monks made **pilgrimages** to India to bring back sacred texts, helping Buddhism to flourish in China. European monks journeyed east to try to convert the Mongols to Christianity. Travelers along the Silk Road encountered these religions, along with Islam, Hinduism, and Zoroastrianism, and in many cases, brought knowledge of these faiths back home with them, where they were able to put down new roots.

In addition to silk, tea, spices, jade, glassware and silverware, gold, perfumes, wool, and horses were traded from region to region along these routes. Technology, too, traveled the Silk Road. It is a certainty that another great Chinese invention—paper—was introduced to the world via the Silk Road. It is highly likely that gunpowder and weapon technology also left China to travel these global pathways. In whatever new places gunpowder was adopted, inventors found new and improved ways to harness its explosive power.

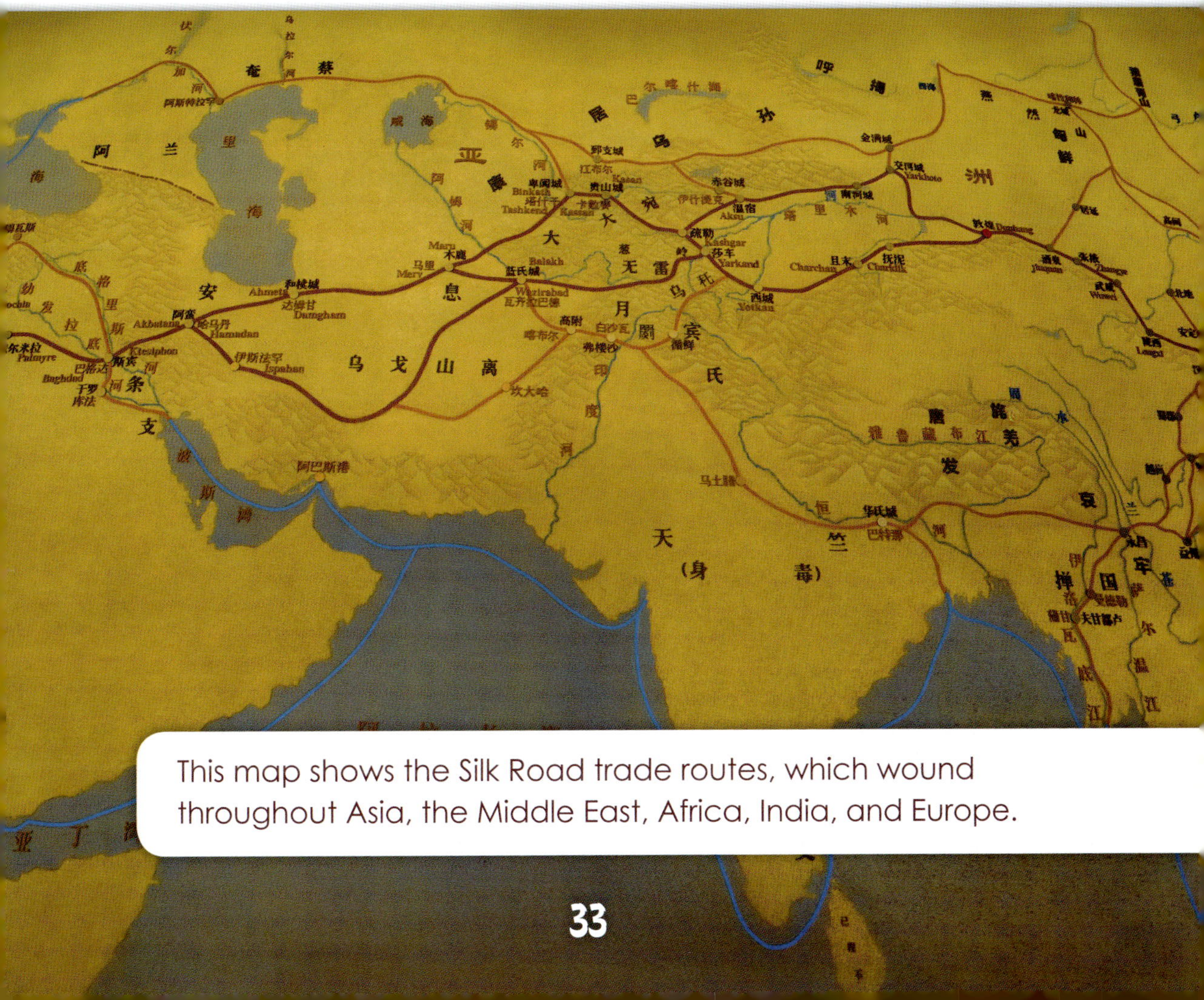

This map shows the Silk Road trade routes, which wound throughout Asia, the Middle East, Africa, India, and Europe.

A Secret No More

It is not clear how knowledge of gunpowder spread throughout the world. Most likely, it was a combination of the Silk Road and the Mongol invasions. But what is clear is that by the middle to late thirteenth century, gunpowder—or at least knowledge of it—had arrived in Japan, Southeast Asia, India, Europe, and the Middle East. References to it would start being made in Korea and Russia in the fourteenth century.

Hasan al-Rammah was an Arab chemist and the first person in the Middle East to describe gunpowder. He also explained a way to purify saltpeter, sketched the first torpedo, and invented new types of gunpowder, fuses, and lighters. His knowledge of gunpowder may have come from India, but Hasan al-Rammah knew that the ultimate source of the technology was China. His words for saltpeter, rockets, and fireworks were "Chinese snow," "Chinese flowers," and "Chinese arrows," respectively.

The first reference to gunpowder in Europe was made by the English natural philosopher Roger Bacon. He was friends with William of Rubruck, a fellow Franciscan friar. William was appointed missionary to the Mongols by King Louis IX of France and wrote a very detailed report for him about his travels, including a lengthy description of the Mongols and their customs. It seems likely that gunpowder and gunpowder weapons would have been mentioned in this report's discussion of Mongol warfare practices. Bacon may have derived his knowledge of gunpowder from William's observations.

Roger Bacon, a thirteenth-century friar and philosopher, was the first European to describe gunpowder.

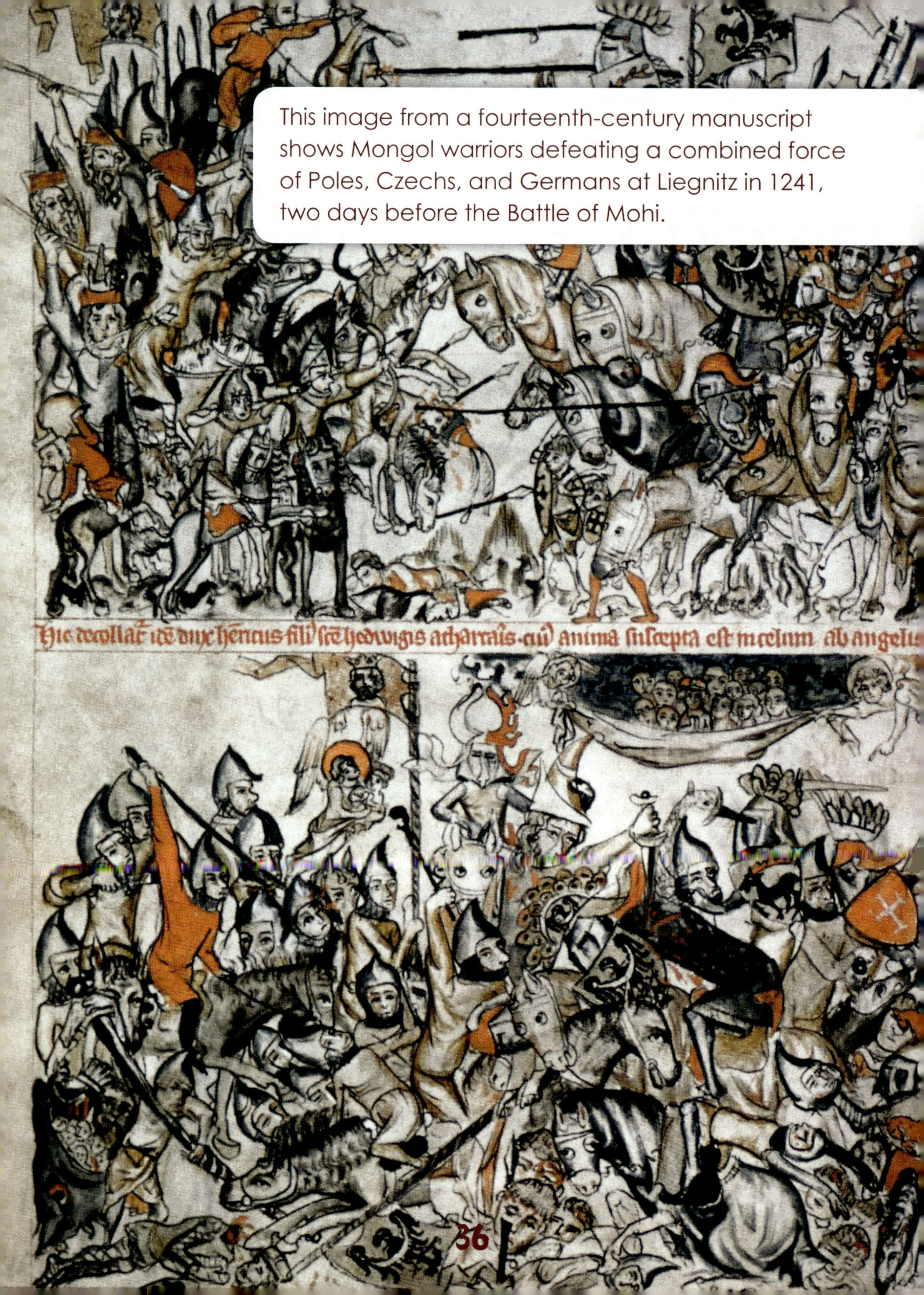

This image from a fourteenth-century manuscript shows Mongol warriors defeating a combined force of Poles, Czechs, and Germans at Liegnitz in 1241, two days before the Battle of Mohi.

Another way that Europe may have been introduced to gunpowder and gunpowder-based weaponry was through the Battle of Mohi in 1241. This was the most important battle between the Mongol Empire and the Kingdom of Hungary during the Mongol invasion of Europe. Contemporary accounts describe the Mongol use of "flaming arrows" and "naphtha bombs" against the Hungarian forces. Naphtha is a flammable liquid hydrocarbon mixture that can be made of petroleum, natural gas, coal tar, pitch, or peat.

Adopting their enemy's technology as they encountered it during their conquest of other parts of China, the Mongols are believed to have, in turn, used gunpowder weapons during their invasion of India. Following the Mongol invasions, there are references to dazzling pyrotechnic displays, military rockets, and elephant-mounted flamethrowers in Indian sources. The first reference to a firearm in India occurred in 1366, and gunpowder weapons were commonly used during battles and sieges in the 1400s.

It is believed that both Mongol warriors (during the invasion of Java in 1293) and Arab Silk Road traders brought gunpowder technology and cannons to the Indonesian archipelago. Korea is thought to have acquired its knowledge of gunpowder when a Korean scholar paid a Chinese merchant to give him the secret explosive formula.

Early Modern Weaponry

While gunpowder was spreading around the world, the Chinese continued to innovate. The Ming Dynasty rose to power in 1368, partly on the strength of founder Zhu Yuanzhang's effective use of gunpowder weapons, including guns. Ming-era guns and cannons were small—ranging from about 6 pounds (3 kg) to 165 pounds (75 kg)—and were not very accurate, with a small range (about 150 feet, or 45 meters). Yet

Starting in the sixteenth century, China began adopting European-style weapons, including the new handguns known as the arquebus and the musket. Especially valuable were the large new artillery pieces, which could weigh more than 5 tons (4,500 kg) and fire 300-pound (136 kg) cannon balls. These weapons were so powerful and destructive that they changed the design of defensive structures. Fortresses became star-shaped, with thicker walls, and artillery rooms were built where cannons could be fired out of windows.

they began to use iron rather than stone balls, which increased the firearm's destructive power. Beginning in the late fourteenth century, the dampening, compressing, and drying of gunpowder into cakes allowed the Chinese to create more explosive land mines and to fire projectiles several hundred yards.

The last great Chinese firearms innovation of the early modern period was the "great divine cannon." This was a large iron gun that weighed over 1,300 pounds (600 kg) and fired 10-pound (5 kg) lead balls. It could actually fire several cannon balls at once, along with a hundred smaller iron shots.

A fifteenth-century soldier fires off an arquebus, an early version of a long gun or rifle.

Constructive Gunpowder

Gunpowder's explosive force had many uses other than military. In fact, its destructive power could actually be quite constructive! Because of its unique blasting ability, gunpowder was used by civil engineers to build much of the **infrastructure** that allowed the world to modernize. China was using gunpowder as early as 1541 to rebuild and improve the Grand Canal, the human-made "river" that connects the Yellow and Yangtze Rivers.

In 1865, when Charles Crocker, the chief of construction for the western half of America's Transcontinental Railroad, was faced with a labor shortage, he decided to turn to Chinese immigrants to help him. Crocker said that if the Chinese invented gunpowder, they would know how to build this railroad. The Chinese laborers worked 12 hours a day, six days a week, earning a reputation for being very reliable workers. By 1867, 12,000 of the Central Pacific Railroad's 13,500 employees were Chinese immigrants.

Gunpowder revolutionized the mining industry. Previous to its use, large rocks had to be broken up by hand or heated in large fires and then rapidly quenched with water. This involved an enormous amount of labor, time, and expense. Similarly, gunpowder made quarrying, road construction, and railroad construction—including tunneling—far faster, easier, and less expensive.

Starting in the mid-nineteenth century, other explosives were developed for blasting and **propellant** purposes. For both military and civil engineering applications, gunpowder began to be replaced by dynamite, nitroglycerin, nitrocellulose, and smokeless powders.

Today, gunpowder is still used in power tools, like rivet guns, cable splicers, and stud guns. It is also the propellant used in stun guns.

Chinese and European immigrants used both gunpowder and nitroglycerine to clear away all obstacles to the tracks of the Transcontinental Railroad.

Celebrate China!

There is one thing that gunpowder is still used for all around the world—fireworks! No public celebration is complete without them. Many holidays and festivals—like the Lunar New Year and the Fourth of July—feature fireworks to enhance the festivities and provoke wonder and awe. Gunpowder, so often associated with destruction, has found its most creative and joyful use in firework displays of breathtaking color, light, and sound.

Today, 99 percent of the fireworks that ordinary Americans buy and 70 percent of the fireworks used in professional displays come from China. The biggest producer of fireworks in the world is a city in China called Liuyang in Hunan Province. There are about a thousand firework factories in the city. Together, they make 60 percent of the fireworks that China exports and sells worldwide. Americans alone spend almost $1 billion on fireworks every year.

We have China to thank for fireworks and firecrackers. Loud, startling noises were thought to be able to scare off evil spirits. So beginning around 200 BCE in China, people began lighting pieces of bamboo on fire. Air pockets in the bamboo would explode, creating a loud popping noise. After the Chinese had invented gunpowder, they began stuffing it in hollowed-out bamboo to create even louder blasts. Soon they were attaching pyrotechnic devices to arrows and firing them up in the air. When the formula for gunpowder was adjusted to be more explosive, they were able to fire off pyrotechnic rockets—the first true firework display!

Fireworks light the night sky over Shanghai during the opening ceremonies of the World Expo.

Glossary

alchemist A person who studied a medieval-era form of chemistry and natural philosophy and who hoped to turn base metals into gold, find a single cure for all diseases, and achieve the secret to prolonged or eternal life.

ambitious Having a desire to achieve a particular goal; aspiring.

civil engineering The design and construction of public works, such as bridges, tunnels, railroads, highways, and harbors.

elixir A substance that was thought to be able to change base metals into gold and/or provide for prolonged or eternal life; a cure for all diseases.

firearm A weapon from which a shot is fired and propelled by gunpowder; usually refers to a small weapon, like a handgun or rifle.

flammable Able to be ignited easily and burned quickly.

formula A recipe or prescription; a set of instructions for making something from various ingredients.

incendiary Able to ignite flammable materials; also, a weapon, such as a bomb, designed to start a fire.

infrastructure The system of public works of a town, state, or country, such as roads, highways, tunnels, bridges, airports, railways and rail stations, buildings, etc.

innovation A new idea, method, or device; the introduction of something new.

natural philosophy The study of nature and the physical universe from a spiritual or philosophical perspective; natural philosophy evolved into the natural and physical sciences.

pilgrimage A journey taken to a shrine or sacred place by people devoted to a certain religion or belief system.

projectile A self-propelled weapon, such as a rocket; a missile that carries and delivers an explosive or incendiary weapon.

propellant An explosive for hurling projectiles.

pyrotechnic A firework; something that ignites a rocket or produces an explosion; the combustible substance used in a firework, such as gunpowder.

shrapnel A projectile that has a gunpowder charge and encases lead balls; when the projectile explodes, the casing falls away and the lead balls are hurled through the air at intended targets. Also, the deadly fragments created by exploding bombs, mines, or shells.

siege A military blockade of a city or fortress, intended to force that city's or fortress's surrender; a persistent, heavy attack.

For More Information

Asia Society (three locations)
725 Park Avenue
New York, NY 10021
(212) 288-6400

1370 Southmore Boulevard
Houston, TX 77004

9 Justice Drive
Admiralty Hong Kong
852-2103-9511
Website: https://asiasociety.org
Asia Society is the leading educational organization dedicated to promoting mutual understanding and strengthening partnerships among people, leaders, and institutions of Asia and the United States in a global context.

Chinese Historical Society of America
965 Clay Street
San Francisco, CA 94108
(415) 391-1188, ext. 101
Website: https://chsa.org
The Chinese Historical Society of America is the oldest organization in the country dedicated to the interpretation, promotion, and preservation of the social, cultural, and political history and contributions of the Chinese in America.

Institute of Civil Engineers (ICE)
1 Great George Street, Westminster
London, UK SW1P 3AA
Website: https://www.ice.org.uk
ICE helps the civil engineering industry learn and share knowledge so that civil engineers can better maintain the natural and built environment. ICE also promotes the essential contributions that civil engineers make to society worldwide and seeks to attract and train the next generation of creative and talented civil engineers.

The Military Museum of the Chinese People's Revolution
9 Fuxing Road
Haidian District
Beijing, China 100038
Website: http://eng.jb.mil.cn
This museum's collection of cultural relics reflects the military history of ancient and modern China and the military history of the world. The museum currently houses over 180,000 cultural relics, including aircraft, artillery, ships, missiles, guns, ammunition, medals, badges, seals, coins, pottery, porcelain, utensils, clothing, flags, documents, and notes.

Museum of Chinese in America
215 Centre Street
New York, NY 10013
(855) 955-MOCA
Website: http://www.mocanyc.org
Founded in 1980, the Museum of Chinese in America (MOCA) is dedicated to preserving and presenting the history, heritage, culture, and diverse experiences of people of Chinese descent in the United States.

National Museum of China (NMC)
No. 16 East Chang'an Street
Dongcheng District
Beijing, China 100006
Website: http://en.chnmuseum.cn
The NMC is a palace of history and art reflecting and displaying China's traditional and modern culture. It houses more than 1.4 million objects that typify and bear witness to the richness and depth of China's 5,000-year-old civilization.

For Further Reading

Andrade, Tonio. *The Gunpowder Age: China, Military Innovation, and the Rise of the West in World History*. Princeton, NJ: Princeton University Press, 2017.

Andrade, Tonio. *The Lost Colony: The Untold Story of China's First Great Victory Over the West*. Princeton, NJ: Princeton University Press, 2013.

Bardoe, Cheryl, and the Field Museum. *China: A History*. New York, NY: Harry N. Abrams, 2019.

Cotterell, Arthur. *Ancient China*. New York, NY: DK Eyewitness, 2005.

Culp, Jennifer. *Ancient Chinese Technology*. New York, NY: Rosen Publishing, 2016.

Field, Simon Quellen. *Boom! The Chemistry and History of Explosives*. Chicago, IL: Chicago Review Press, 2017.

Frankopan, Peter. *The Silk Roads: A New History of the World*. New York, NY: Bloomsbury Publishing, 2015.

Hanson-Harding, Brian. *Ancient Chinese Religion and Beliefs*. New York, NY: Rosen Publishing, 2016.

Harrison-Hall, Jessica. *China: A History in Objects*. London, UK: Thames & Hudson, 2018.

Hurt, Avery Elizabeth. *Ancient Chinese Government and Geography*. New York, NY: Rosen Publishing, 2016.

Liu, Jing. *Barbarians and the Birth of Chinese Identity: The Five Dynasties and Ten Kingdoms to the Yuan Dynasty (907–1368)* (Understanding China Through Comics). Berkeley, CA: Stone Bridge Press, 2017.

Liu, Jing. *Division to Unification in Imperial China: The Three Kingdoms to the Tan Dynasty (220–907)* (Understanding China Through Comics). Berkeley, CA: Stone Bridge Press, 2016.

Liu, Jing. *Foundations of Chinese Civilization: The Yellow Emperor to the Han Dynasty (2697 BCE–220 CE)* (Understanding China Through Comics). Berkeley, CA: Stone Bridge Press, 2016.

Liu, Jing. *The Making of Modern China: The Ming Dynasty to the Qing Dynasty (1368–1912)* (Understanding China Through Comics). Berkeley, CA: Stone Bridge Press, 2017.

Lusted, Marcia Amidon. *Ancient Chinese Daily Life*. New York, NY: Rosen Publishing, 2016.

Morrow, Paula. *Ancient Chinese Culture*. New York, NY: Rosen Publishing, 2016.

Sun Tzu. *The Art of War* (translated by Peter Harris). New York, NY: Alfred A. Knopf, 2018.

Wasserstrom, Jeffrey N., ed. *The Oxford Illustrated History of Modern China*. New York, NY: Oxford University Press, 2018.

Bibliography

Andrade, Tonio. *The Gunpowder Age: China, Military Innovation, and the Rise of the West in World History*. Princeton, NJ: Princeton University Press, 2017.

Beckwith, Christopher I. *Empires of the Silk Road: A History of Central Eurasia from the Bronze Age to the Present*. Princeton, NJ: Princeton University Press, 2009.

Brown, G. I. *The Big Bang: A History of Explosives*. Stroud, UK: Sutton Publishing, 1998.

Chase, Kenneth. *Firearms: A Global History to 1700*. New York, NY: Cambridge University Press, 2003.

Cressy, David. *Saltpeter: The Mother of Gunpowder*. New York, NY: Oxford University Press, 2013.

Crosby, Alfred W. *Throwing Fire: Projectile Technology Through History*. New York, NY: Cambridge University Press, 2002.

Field, Simon Quellen. *Boom! The Chemistry and History of Explosives*. Chicago, IL: Chicago Review Press, 2017.

Frankopan, Peter. *The Silk Roads: A New History of the World*. New York, NY: Bloomsbury Publishing, 2015.

Horsley, Scott. "For Independence Day Fireworks, U.S. Depends on China." NPR.org. 2018. https://www.npr.org/2018/07/03/625405653/for-independence-day-fireworks-u-s-depends-on-china.

Kelly, Jack. *Gunpowder: Alchemy, Bombards, and Pyrotechnics: The History of the Explosive That Changed the World*. New York, NY: Basic Books, 2005.

Khan, Iqtidar Alam. *Gunpowder and Firearms: Warfare in Medieval India*. New York, NY: Oxford University Press, 2004.

Lorge, Peter A. *The Asian Military Revolution: From Gunpowder to the Bomb*. New York, NY: Cambridge University Press, 2008.

Mote, Frederick W. *Imperial China: 900–1800*. Cambridge, MA: Harvard University Press, 1999.

Partington, J. R. *A History of Greek Fire and Gunpowder*. Baltimore, MD: Johns Hopkins University Press, 1999.

Ropp, Paul S. *China in World History*. New York, NY: Oxford University Press, 2010.

SilkRoad.com. "Gun and Gunpowder." Undated. Retrieved February 2020. http://www.silk-road.com/artl/gun.shtml.

Szczepanski, Kallie. "The Invention of Gunpowder: A History." ThoughtCo. 2019. https://www.thoughtco.com/invention-of-gunpowder-195160.

Tang, Cindy. "Chinese New Year Firecrackers." China Highlights. Undated. Retrieved February 2020. https://www.chinahighlights.com/travelguide/festivals/chinese-new-year-firecrackers.htm.

Veverka, Jesse. "Liuyang—You'll Get a Bang Out of the Fireworks There." CNN Travel. 2017. https://www.cnn.com/travel/article/liuyang-china-fireworks-born/index.html.

Whipps, Heather. "How Gunpowder Changed the World." LiveScience. 2008. https://www.livescience.com/7476-gunpowder-changed-world.html).

Index